T

St. Helens Libraries

Please return / renew this item by the last date shown.
Books may be renewed by phone and Internet.

Telephone - (01744) 676954 or 677822
Email - centrallibrary@sthelens.gov.uk
Online - sthelens.gov.uk/librarycatalogue
Twitter - twitter.com/STHLibraries

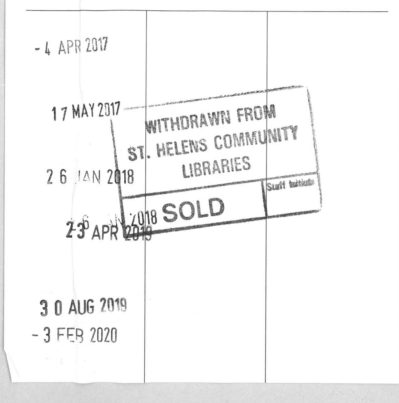

- 4 APR 2017

17 MAY 2017

WITHDRAWN FROM
ST. HELENS COMMUNITY
LIBRARIES

2 6 JAN 2018

Staff Initials

2018 SOLD

2 3 APR 2019

3 0 AUG 2019

- 3 FEB 2020

D0359058

3 8056 3501 0 0931

FACT CAT

ELECTRICITY

Izzi Howell

WAYLAND
www.waylandbooks.co.uk

FACT CAT

Get your paws on this fantastic new mega-series from Wayland!

Join our Fact Cat on a journey of fun learning about every subject under the sun!

First published in Great Britain in 2017 by Wayland
Copyright © Hodder and Stoughton Limited, 2017

All rights reserved

ISBN: 978 1 5263 0178 9

10 9 8 7 6 5 4 3 2 1

FSC
www.fsc.org

MIX
Paper from
responsible sources
FSC® C104740

Wayland
An imprint of Hachette Children's Group
Part of Hodder & Stoughton
Carmelite House
50 Victoria Embankment
London EC4Y 0DZ

An Hachette UK Company
www.hachette.co.uk
www.hachettechildrens.co.uk

A catalogue for this title is available from
the British Library
Printed and bound in China

Produced for Wayland by
White-Thomson Publishing Ltd
www.wtpub.co.uk

Editor: Izzi Howell
Design: Clare Nicholas
Fact Cat illustrations: Shutterstock/Julien Troneur
Consultant: Karina Philip

Picture and illustration credits:
Alamy: Image Source 18; iStock: Smileus 8, vladoskan 20, yourth 21; Peter Bull: 11; Shutterstock: Eric Boucher cover, John-Kelly title page and 6, Sailorr 4, Stefano Garau 5, Neil Mitchell 7, Aerovista Luchtfotografie 9, Syda Productions 10, Dmytro Vietrov 12, BlueRingMedia 13, ULKASTUDIO 14, Bohbeh 15, Radu Bercan 16, Sergey Nivens 17, Sorbis 19t, Sinisa Botas 19b.

Every effort has been made to clear copyright. Should there be any inadvertent omission, please apply to the publisher for rectification.

The author, Izzi Howell, is a writer and editor specialising in children's educational publishing.

The consultant, Karina Philip, is a teacher and a primary literacy consultant with an MA in creative writing.

Warning: Electricity is dangerous. Do not touch or play with electrical wire, plugs or sockets.

FACT CAT FACT

There is a question for you to answer on most spreads in this book. You can check your answers on page 24.

St.Helens Library Services

3805535018093	
PETERS	21-Feb-2017
537	£11.99

CONTENTS

WHAT IS ELECTRICITY?

Electricity is a type of energy. We use electricity to **power** many objects in our homes, such as computers, fridges and lights.

FACT CAT FACT

Electricity travels very fast. It can move 3 million metres in one second!

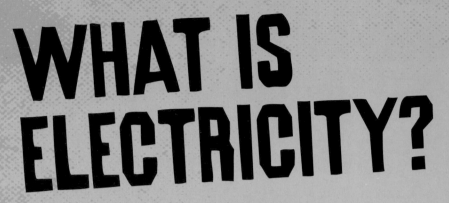

We use electricity to power large machines, such as trains. Which other forms of transport can be powered by electricity?

Electrical appliances are powered by **current electricity**. This is a type of electricity that we make. It can move along wires from one place to another.

Lightning is a type of natural electricity called **static electricity** (see page 18). The static electricity stays up in the clouds until it shoots down to the ground as lightning.

MAKING ELECTRICITY

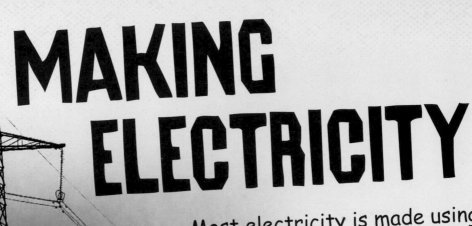

Most electricity is made using huge machines in **power stations**. Then, it is sent through long wires to homes and buildings.

wire

The electricity in these wires is dangerous and very strong. Metal towers hold up the wires so that they are far from the ground. Find out the name of these towers.

To make electricity, the power station first burns a **fuel**, such as **coal**. They use the heat to **boil** water, which makes **steam**. Then, the steam makes a **turbine** wheel spin around. Finally, the spinning turbine powers a **generator**, which makes electricity.

After electricity has been made, the leftover steam is placed in large towers to cool down. Some of it escapes into the air.

FACT CAT FACT

Power stations that burn fuel are bad for the **environment**. This is because burning fuel makes a **gas** called **carbon dioxide**, which can damage the Earth.

7

SUN, WIND AND WATER

We can also make electricity using sunlight, wind and water. It is better for the environment to make electricity in these ways.

Some people use **solar panels** to make electricity to use in their house. Solar panels contain a material that makes electricity when the sun shines on it.

Making electricity from wind or water is similar to making electricity in a power station. Instead of using steam to push the turbine, the movement of wind or water makes the turbine spin.

Wind turbines are often placed along the coast or at sea, where there is lots of wind. What is the name of a group of wind turbines?

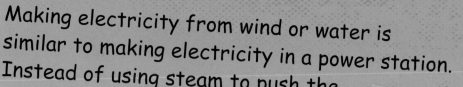

FACT CAT FACT

People have made energy from wind and water for hundreds of years. In the past, people used windmills and watermills to grind flour and power simple machines.

negative side

positive side

CIRCUITS

A circuit is a path around which electricity can travel. In a circuit, there are always wires and a power source, such as a battery. You can also add other parts, such as lamps.

Batteries have two sides – the positive side and the negative side. They have to be placed the right way around. Can you name two objects in your house that use batteries?

In a circuit, electricity comes out of the battery. It flows through the wires and back into the battery. This electricity powers any lamps or **buzzers** that are in the circuit.

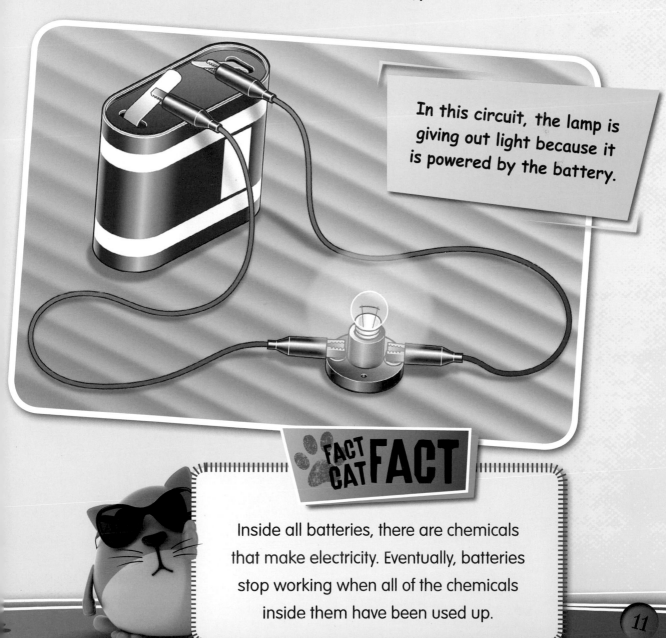

In this circuit, the lamp is giving out light because it is powered by the battery.

FACT CAT FACT

Inside all batteries, there are chemicals that make electricity. Eventually, batteries stop working when all of the chemicals inside them have been used up.

SWITCHES AND CIRCUITS

Most electrical appliances have switches. Switches stop and start the flow of electricity through a circuit.

Switching off lights when you leave a room helps to save electricity. It also saves money, as you have to pay to use electricity.

In a circuit, electricity only flows if a switch is closed and the circuit is complete, with no gaps. If the switch is open, no electricity will flow.

In this circuit, the lamp is giving out light because the switch is closed. What would happen to the lamp if you opened the switch?

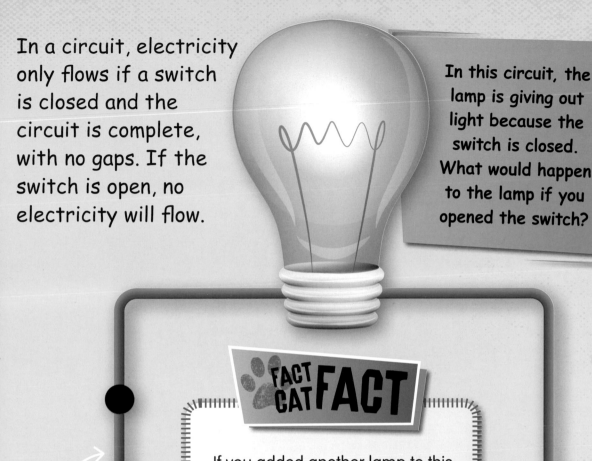

switch

FACT CAT FACT

If you added another lamp to this circuit, the electricity from the battery would be split between the two lamps. Both lamps would give out less light.

CONDUCTORS AND INSULATORS

Electrical **conductors** are materials that let electricity pass through them. Most metals are electrical conductors, such as copper and iron.

copper

The wires in a circuit have to conduct electricity, so they are made from copper.

Electrical **insulators** do not let electricity pass through them. Some examples of electrical insulators are wood, plastic and glass. Insulators are important in a circuit, as they stop electricity from escaping.

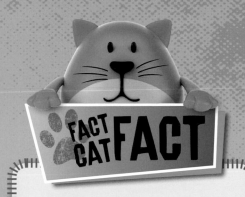

FACT CAT FACT

In some countries, plugs have two pins and in others, they have three.

pins

The outside of a plug is covered with plastic so that it is safe to hold. Why are the pins of a plug made from metal?

Plugs and **sockets** are dangerous. Do not play with them.

ELECTRICAL SAFETY

Electricity is useful but it can also be very dangerous. A small amount of electricity can give you a painful **electric shock**. A lot of electricity can kill you.

This sign means that there is powerful electricity on the other side of the fence. Never touch any outdoor electrical switches or wires.

FACT CAT FACT

Electricity can pass through water. This is why it is very dangerous to get an electrical appliance wet or to touch one with wet hands. Why shouldn't you go in the sea during a thunderstorm?

Electricity can conduct through different materials, so you should never put anything other than a plug inside an electric socket. The electricity might travel through the object into your body.

Always fly kites far away from overhead electrical wires. If the kite touches the wire, the electricity can travel down the kite string and give you an electric shock.

AMAZING ELECTRICITY

Static electricity can make things stick together. For example, if you rub a balloon on your hair, it creates static electricity that will make the balloon stick to a wall.

Static electricity can make your hair stand on end. To try this out, rub a balloon on your hair and then hold the balloon near your head.

FACT CAT FACT

You can bend water with static electricity. If you rub a comb through your hair and then hold the comb next to a running tap, the stream of water will bend.

Some gases glow a bright colour when electricity passes through them. We can use these gases in bright fluorescent (say flur-es-ent) lights and plasma balls to make coloured light.

Fluorescent signs are made from glass tubes filled with special gases. When they are connected to electricity, the gases glow.

There is an electrical current inside this plasma ball. When you touch the ball, the electricity comes to your finger because your body conducts electricity.

ELECTRICITY AND ANIMALS

All animals, including humans, make small amounts of electricity. This electricity sends signals around our body, telling it what to do.

Sharks can **sense** the electricity in other animals. This helps them to find fish to eat. Which part of the body do sharks use to sense electricity?

Some animals can make large amounts of electricity. Electric eels send out electricity to hurt and kill their **prey**.

The electric eel lives in rivers in the rainforests of South America.

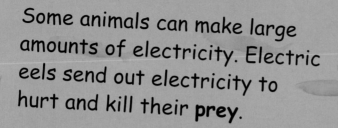

FACT CAT FACT

An electric eel can create an electric shock that is several times stronger than the electricity in a socket.

QUIZ

Try to answer the questions below. Look back through the book to help you. Check your answers on page 24.

1 Most electricity is made in power stations. True or not true?

a) true

b) not true

2 Which of these parts supplies electricity in a circuit?

a) wire

b) battery

c) lamp

3 If a switch is open, electricity flows through the circuit. True or not true?

a) true

b) not true

4 Which material conducts electricity?

a) copper

b) wood

c) plastic

5 It is dangerous to fly kites near overhead wires. True or not true?

a) true

b) not true

6 Which animal senses electricity?

a) rabbit

b) chicken

c) shark

GLOSSARY

boil when a liquid is boiled, it reaches a temperature when it makes bubbles and steam

buzzer an electrical device that makes a sound

carbon dioxide a gas that is made when fuel is burned that is bad for the environment

coal a hard black substance that can be burned

conductor something that lets electricity pass through

current electricity electricity that can move along wires from one place to another

electric shock a sudden painful feeling that you get when electricity passes through your body

environment the air, water and land where living things live

fuel something that is burned to make heat or power

gas something that is neither a solid nor a liquid, such as air

generator a machine that makes electricity

insulator something that does not let electricity pass through

power to supply energy to a machine and make it work

power station a factory where electricity is made

prey an animal that is hunted and killed by another animal

sense to feel or experience something

socket the place in the wall where you can connect a cable to the electrical supply

solar panel a machine that turns light from the Sun into electricity

static electricity electricity that stays in one place

steam gas made when water boils

turbine a large machine that makes electricity by turning a wheel

INDEX

ANSWERS

Pages 4–21

Page 4: Trams or electric cars

Page 6: Pylon

Page 9: Wind farm

Page 10: Some appliances include TV remotes, clocks and torches.

Page 13: It would stop giving out light.

Page 15: So that the electricity from the socket can pass through into the wire.

Page 16: Because if the lightning hits the water, it can travel to you and give you an electric shock.

Page 20: Nose

Quiz answers

1   true

2   b – battery

3   not true – electricity only flows through a complete circuit with a closed switch.

4   a – copper

5   true

6   c – shark

OTHER TITLES IN THE FACT CAT SERIES...

WAYLAND
www.waylandbooks.co.uk